Your Authority Book:

Define Your Unique Solution

RUTH SULLIVAN

DEDICATION

(This is a great space to recognise or thank someone who has helped or supported you to get where you are today.)

CONTENTS

ACKNOWLEDGMENTS

Here you have plenty of space to thank colleagues, friends and/or family, and to recognize those people who have been part of your journey so far, co – authored or contributed to your book.

FOREWORD

The Foreword is a great place to place a high – profile personal recommendation for you and/or your work.

You can use a glowing testimonial from a satisfied customer or a recommendation from an established figure in your niche – someone whose name already commands authority and respect from your target audience.

If that person is particularly well – known, you can highlight 'Foreword by A.N. Other' on the cover and alongside your Amazon sales copy.

Inviting a well – known client or important figure in your niche not only lends weight to your book, but also brings the additional bonuses:

1. You bring your work to the attention of that respected authority figure or valued client and let them know that you are publishing a book.

2. Your name is associated with the name of that well – known personality or company in your book marketing.

3. When invited to write a Foreword, most people are honoured to be asked and happy to oblige.

Be sure to promise that you will send them a complimentary copy and, if applicable, that their name will appear on the cover.

If they read the contents—or even just skim through the chapter titles – they will learn more about you, your services and the unique benefits of working with you.

4. They tell their peers and clients that they have been asked to write the foreword to your book, thus generating interest in you and your work.

5. Their name will appear alongside the publicity for the book as 'with Foreword by…' and be seen by anyone who buys or reads the book, resulting in free publicity for them and their work.

It's a win – win situation!

Ruth Sullivan,
Publication Consultant,
Bergamo, Italy 2017

"A man may speak with his tongue and be heard around the corner; but another man may speak with his pen and be heard around the globe."

James Lendall Basford (1845 – 1915)

INTRODUCTION

Have you noticed how the title of 'published author' confers instant credibility?

Perhaps you have observed how other consultants and coaches, who don't appear to be any better qualified or any more experienced than you, can effortlessly leverage the power of the printed word to get their work in front of potential clients and respected influencers in their niche?

Their book opens up doors to speaking invitations, joint ventures, press articles etc. and they become more visible to their ideal clients.

How does that make you feel? Inadequate, frustrated, resentful, envious? If you experience any of those feelings, you can be sure that, somewhere deep inside, you know that you have the ability to do the same – and that you should!

In publishing your work, you have the opportunity to explain exactly what you do and how you deliver your solution. **You stand out from the crowd of similar providers by defining what makes you unique.**

Not only do you gain respect and authority and get noticed for what you do, you have a detailed description of the service you offer; a clearly presented statement of what you stand for and who you serve.

Many coaches and consultants lament the fact that they have to spend so much time generating leads for their business, endlessly attempting to convince potential clients to hire them. Much of this time could be saved if they were able to present a succinct and well – defined description of their unique solution in the form of their authority book.

It has become popular to offer an e.book as a pdf for download, but an electronic file does does not carry the same perceived value as a printed **physical book,** nor does it hold the same potential to boost your online profile and drive your offline marketing. Although, when you have your book published, it's very easy to produce an electronic version to be offered alongside your book on Amazon, or as a download on your website.

The argument for distilling the essence of what you do is strong, and you have seen how it works for other people, so what is stopping you?

There are many limiting beliefs around publishing and self – publishing, so the purpose of this book is to help you to examine which beliefs you hold and whether they still serve you.

Because traditional publishing has been governed by publishing houses and the requirement to hire a publishing agent, the misconception that publishing is elitist or a long – term investment of time has prevented many from seeing their work in print.

However, the advent of self – publishing has removed the limiting factor of the publishing houses, and opened up exciting opportunities for showcasing the unique solution you offer.

Today's online marketing platforms and social media sites allow little time or space to present your ideas clearly in one place, but a book gives you a forum on which to explain exactly who you are, what you do and who you serve.

There has never been a better time to publish your book, to present your ideas, describe what sets you apart and get your best work in front of the people who matter to you.

It is my intention to inspire you by showing you how your book might look and to challenge the limiting beliefs you may have concerning your ability to write and publish.

If you believe you have nothing to say, let me tell you, you have!

Every human being has a unique purpose, talent and message to share.

It is my firm conviction that everyone's unique gift is equally valuable and that everyone has been given their gift for a purpose – because it is needed on this planet right now!

Your message is the very core of who you are.

You are not required to share that message with everyone, but you *are* required to deliver that message to a specific group of people who need the exact solution you offer.

They are waiting for that solution – and it is your responsibility to find them.

For some consultants and coaches, their unique purpose is clear, but they are struggling to define precisely what they do. As a result, they are struggling to make contact with the specific group of people who require their services.

For others, who are still functioning under the outmoded 'get a job' strategies which grew out of the Industrial Era, the conditioned instinct to offer their services as 'all things to all men' is actually sabotaging their success.

If that's you, may I present a gentle reminder that the Industrial Era is over!

The Internet is here to stay, it cannot be 'un – invented', and the implications for your business cannot be met with complacency. The 'Jack – of – all – Trades' approach, which was fostered by the limitations of geographical location, no longer applies. The rules have changed–forever!!

That means it no longer makes sense to just copy what someone else is doing and expect to get the same results.

The more people who can do what you do and offer the same results, the less valuable are your services, the more you will subject yourself to the old rules of 'competition', and the more you will struggle to get noticed by your ideal clients.

Your greatest value lies in what makes you unique.

I see many coaches and consultants exhausted and frustrated by the sheer effort of attracting and retaining clients, so that they spend more time coaxing than coaching.

There has to be a better way!

In fact, there is.

Your gift is precious and your time is valuable.

Let's distill your essence, once and for all, on the printed page!

Let it be a clear and comprehensive description of who you are, what you stand for, the unique way you deliver your expertise and the specific group of people you serve.

Different aspects of your work will appeal to different clients. A book allows the reader to focus on the aspects of your solution of greatest interest to them, and leaves them with a physical reference source should they need to refer to the details at a later date.

They may not need your solution right now, but they may do in future!

You have an exciting choice: to continue to pitch your services alongside all the other providers offering similar solutions, or to stand out from the competition by defining what makes you unique.

For when you are unique, there is no competition!

Is it finally time to blast through the excuses that are holding you back from publishing your authority book?

The World is waiting for your Message.

Ruth Sullivan,
Bergamo, Italy
May 2017

"Keep away from people who try to belittle your ambitions. Small people always do that, but the really great make you feel that you, too, can become great."

Mark Twain

CHAPTER 1: WHY PUBLISH A BOOK ?

It has always been said that everyone has a book in them – and that's so true, because everyone has a unique skill set and message to deliver.

So what's holding you back?

Like many people, you have probably realized the value in writing your authority book, but you keep putting it off to 'someday' – and we all know that 'someday' never comes!

You can see the advantages of publishing, but your resistance to actually getting it done will always prevail while your **beliefs** tell you that the pain exceeds the gain.

It is my job, as a publication coach, to shine a light on those beliefs, to help you to see where they came from, and to give you the opportunity to decide whether or not they are still valid.

Your mind is very clever at persuading you that you don't

have the time, that you don't have anything worth saying or that you don't know where to start.

You might think you are acting from modesty or a lack of self – confidence, but there is actually a much more powerful force at work here.

Your subconscious mind is trying to keep you safe.

Why? From what?

Your subconscious mind resists change; it wants to keep you stuck where you are now.

In my work, I have the incredible privilege of guiding first – time authors through to seeing their work in print. Time and time again, I see what happens to people when they write and publish a book:

They change.

In good way! Their self – confidence increases and they go from hiding their light to knowing the value of what they offer. It's almost as if they don't believe their own worth until they actually see it for themselves in black and white!

Your subconscious mind knows that a published book has the potential to bring about massive change in your life.

So now that we have exposed the little saboteur for what it

is, are you ready to shine some fresh light on those little lies it has been feeding you?

The recent developments in self – publishing mean there has never been an easier time to get your book published, and the field is wide open to those who are able to identify the possibilities and who are ready to address the fears holding them back from taking action **now**.

Added to that are the revolutionary changes in the world of work since the advent of the Internet. Many people reacted to these changes negatively, thinking that the move to online working was 'stealing jobs'. That appeared to be the initial effect, but the reality was that the Internet was actually opening up the opportunity for people to create their own work, on their own terms.

However, a couple of centuries of human conditioning to 'get a job', rather than work from your purpose, has left many of us with firmly – entrenched beliefs to which we are still subconsciously clinging.

Prior to the turn of the century, it was possible to just choose a job title and follow what everyone else was doing. The limitations of geographical location meant you only had to stand out from the competition in your local market. In a small pool of similar providers, it paid to offer a range of services to appeal to as many local clients as possible.

You had to diversify to thrive. You became a 'generalist'.

However, the Internet is shaking up the rules of the market. Very few businesses can still operate by applying the 'big fish in a small pond' strategy, and the 'generalist' risks sliding into obscurity among the thousands, or even millions, of similar providers marketing their services online. The rise of the Internet has made it increasingly more difficult to stand out from the competition.

Many consultants and coaches have been slow to adjust to this sea change in the world of work, and are continuing to apply the old 'spread the net wide' approach to their business model. They are still governed by the old pre – internet belief that offering as many services as possible would increase their value and their potential to grow their business.

In fact, today the opposite is the case.

The Internet requires you to be a specialist.

If you are still trying to be 'all things to all men' in the hope that it will improve your chances of success, you are probably, right now, overwhelmed by the constant scramble to get noticed online.

How much of your time is spent competing for keywords, trying to get Google to notice your website, attracting traffic to your webpages? How much fresh content and updating do these pages need? How much effort goes into your Social Media campaigns and promotion?

It can all seem overwhelming, frustrating and, frankly, exhausting, but, most importantly, all this time marketing is eating into the time you want to be investing in your business and actually **doing** what you do best!

This is not new – it has always been true. Look at the world of employment, for example. The more people who can do a job, the less it pays. If you are in a job where you could easily be replaced by virtually anyone, you are unlikely to be earning much. Your salary increases as your 'replaceability' decreases.

Your greatest value lies in what makes you unique, and your earning capacity increases with your ability to define that.

Many consultants and coaches are failing to express precisely what they do; to define what problems they solve and for whom.

Unless you do the work to get clear on what makes your products or services unique, you will continue to compete on pricing against a host of other similar providers, and commit yourself and your business to a future of constantly trying to get noticed above the background noise online.

There are three main ways a book can help you to get you and your work noticed, even in what appears to be a competitive market:

- Describe what makes you or your company unique

- Raise your online profile

- Power your offline marketing

Describe what makes you and/or your company unique.

With so many competitors appearing to offer the same, or similar, solutions, it is more important than ever to be able to refine your niche.

Everyone seems to be offering the same format – and a similar blanket approach of 'we do everything for everyone'. In that environment, the consumer's choice is dictated by who has the more aggressive marketing campaign and budget, or who can offer the lowest **price** for the same service – what other determining factor can the consumer apply?

You know you offer a specific, tailor – made solution, but, unless you are able to describe exactly what that is, how can your potential clients understand what you can do for them?

Your values, ideas, experience, and the particular way in which you deliver your service – and to whom – set you apart. You have done great work – and you have many satisfied clients who would testify to that.

Isn't it worth taking the time to define those qualities and to express them clearly?

The online world demands that you present all that information in a few seconds – and grab the attention of the reader – before they move on to the next provider.

A book allows you so much more scope than a business card or a website Homepage to present a more complete picture of what you provide.

Raise your online profile, as a 'published author'

Get your work and your unique ideas and services in front of the top influencers – the movers and shakers in your field – and the ideal clients you would love to work with.

The very fact that you have taken the time to commit your thoughts and expertise to paper shows that you are passionate about what you do.

You are free to express your opinions and thought leadership, as an expert in your niche. You are able to offer valuable insight, drawn from your personal experience, about what is working now, new concepts, trends, etc., and how your approach has solved particular problems for your clients.

Drive your offline marketing

A published book is a physical product. Although it can be marketed and distributed in much the same way as most physical products, its value does not lie primarily in the sales price. In fact, if you want to publish a book in order to make profits from the sales, I would advise strongly against it! You can increase your earnings potential enormously by publishing a book, but rarely through direct sales.

The main objective of your book is to get your work seen – by your ideal clients, and/or by people you would love to work with.

The scramble to promote businesses and services online has left a partial vacuum in the offline world. There is great potential offline to connect with people who need your services and to get the word out about what you do. There are many exciting opportunities to get a copy of your signature book into the hands of your perfect clients.

If you are reading this now – and I have done my research

correctly – you are probably one of my ideal clients. You are doing great things in the world and offering a unique service.

You might even have thought about publishing your authority book before, but, for one reason or another, you have put it off or forgotten about it because you believe it is too difficult or too time – consuming, or you don't know how to go about finding the right person to help you with it.

So you have put the idea on the back burner for now, until you figure out how to do it – one day!

I wrote this book to present the case for publishing your book now – and to show you why the excuses that have been preventing you from taking action and sharing your message with the World – are no longer valid!

"If Moses were alive today he'd come down from the mountain with the Ten Commandments and spend the next five years trying to get them published."

Anonymous

CHAPTER 2: LIMITING BELIEFS

Here are the 7 most common 'beliefs' that people use to put off publishing their authority book until 'someday'.

How many do you recognise?.

1. The publishing process is hard; you have to struggle to convince a publisher to take you on.

2. It's got to be perfect! I'm not good enough to write a book. I'm afraid of being judged as inadequate.

3. I don't know what to write about. I don't have any original idea or revolutionary discovery to unveil!

    I have nothing new or important to say; who would want to read my book?

4. How could my book be marketable? What if nobody buys it – and I'm left with a stack of unsold books to shift?

5. It takes a long time to get a book published. It would be a long – term strategy and I would prefer to concentrate on more immediate marketing strategies that impact my business right now.

6. I've never done it before – I don't know where to start.

7. I don't know who I could get to help me with the logistics. How do I hire Editors. Formatters, Cover designers, etc.?

8. I'm too busy – I don't have the time to stop what I'm doing and write a book. I'll do it someday.

The following chapters are designed to help you re – examine those beliefs and decide whether they still apply.

"An editor is someone who separates the wheat from the chaff and then prints the chaff."

Adlai Stevenson

CHAPTER 3: EXPOSING THE MYTHS

THE LIMITATIONS AND DISADVANTAGES OF TRADITIONAL PUBLISHING

The first five myths concerning publishing a book all stem from the world of traditional publishing.

- The publishing process is hard; you have to struggle to convince a publisher to take you on.

- The book has to be perfect – I'm not good enough,

- I have nothing new or important to write about.

- The subject matter has to be commercially – viable. What if nobody buys the book and I'm left with a stack of unsold copies to shift?

- It takes a long time to get a book published

Up until quite recently, if you wanted to publish a book, the only affordable option was to convince a publishing house to take you on – unless you had a small fortune to invest upfront to fund a private print – run of your project.

However, recent developments in self – publishing have opened up many exciting possibilities, but few people are taking advantage of these opportunities because they are still limited by their own outmoded beliefs about how difficult it is to write and publish a book.

So let's look at each of these myths – and decide whether they are still valid as excuses for not publishing your authority book!

EXCUSE I:
IT'S DIFFICULT TO GET PUBLISHED

We all know the legendary tales about the great authors who were rejected by dozens of publishing houses before they could see their work in print.

The process to get accepted by a publishing house involves hiring an agent and persuading an editorial team that your book concept is marketable.

Unless you are a household name or have a huge Twitter following, a guaranteed market for the book, you will have to convince a traditional publisher that your book is going to sell!

It is this 'prestige' argument – the idea that being accepted by a major publishing house is somehow more prestigious than self – publishing – that has fueled those other excuses that the work has to be perfect, revolutionary, new or a commercial bestseller – in order to be published.

However, if we look at the 'prestige' or 'quality' argument, it doesn't really hold up. Many a poor – quality book has been published simply because the author is well – known or has a guaranteed market for the book. Similarly, many a great book has been rejected because a publisher can't see a market for it.

George Orwell's political allegory "Animal Farm" was rejected by several publishers, most for fear of creating political tensions between Great Britain and the Soviet Union, but one, famously, because "there was no market for animal stories in the USA"!

A publisher's view is subjective and the decision to publish your book is determined by risk.

Having your book accepted by a publishing house is akin to having an insurance company agree to insure your house. You will be accepted if you meet a certain set of logistical parameters that determines whether or not you present a high risk to their recouping their losses and making a profit!

Guy Kawasaki, the former Apple evangelist, now inspirational speaker, entrepreneur and author of 13 books (most of them self – published!), has done much to dispel the myths surrounding the prestige argument for traditional publishing.

He is now a staunch advocate of self – publishing – or, as he prefers to call it 'Artisanal Publishing.".

He responds to the question of whether self – publishing is somehow inferior to traditional publishing thus:

"Would you ever go up to an artisanal baker and ask, "Is the reason why you have your own bakery that you didn't get accepted by a large national baked goods manufacturer?"

(*Source*: www.forbes.com, 21 January, 2013)

"It took me fifteen years to discover I had no talent for writing, but I couldn't give it up because by that time I was too famous."

Robert Benchley

EXCUSE II:

I'M NOT GOOD ENOUGH TO WRITE A BOOK I'M NOT A WRITER

This belief assumes that a book is accepted or rejected for publication on the grounds of **quality**. This is simply not the case.

Commercial viability is the driving factor.

J.K. Rowling had the manuscript for the first Harry Potter book rejected by twelve publishers, before going on to sell 400 million copies in the series and collect numerous awards for her work. She was a risk as an unknown author, until her market was established.

It is vital to understand that 'acceptance' by a publishing house is not a measure of quality and that a published book has to be perfect or the culmination of your life's work.

In fact, 'perfectionism' is not desirable as 'getting it perfect' is often the major barrier to 'getting it done'!

The idea that there are such high stakes in writing a book come from the huge effort and investment of time required to go through the traditional publishing process. It was such a major undertaking that you only wanted to experience it once!

However, after you become familiar with self – publishing, and discover the advantages and possibilities, you will see how easy it is to publish your second, third,...etc.

If you feel that publishing your book will expose you or your work to being criticized, remember that your sternest critics will be acting from envy – and the regret that they did not have the courage or the initiative to do what you are doing!

Leave 'perfection' for your masterpiece – that ultimate 'best of..' tome to be written when you retire, or, at least, when you have that first experience under your belt, and have your message 'out there'.

When you take away the pressure to get it perfect, you free up the space to get it done.

EXCUSE III:

I DON'T HAVE ANYHTING TO WRITE ABOUT

I have no original ideas or revolutionary concepts to reveal.

Your authority book does not require a ground – breaking theory, a textbook thesis or a literary masterpiece. We are talking about your specialist subject, your particular field of expertise. What you do. What service do you provide and what is unique about how you deliver that service to your clients?

This is **your** subject: you could talk about it all day!

The actual writing process is just a matter of translating that passion, those ideas, from your head to the printed page. Fortunately, you no longer need to lock yourself away in a garret and abandon your business while you chain yourself to a desk! There are many ways to make the process not only much easier, but actually enjoyable!

The limiting editorial recommendations and guidelines of traditional publishing houses may require you to compromise your ideas to satisfy the publisher's commercial considerations. They may choose to omit or edit some of your best work in order to appeal to a more general market.

However, self – publishing releases you from the pressure and constraints of getting your work past an editorial committee.

You have complete autonomy over the content of *your* book. After all, no – one knows your target audience or understands your unique solution better than you do!

(N.B. A quick word about presentation editing. You will still need an editor and proof – reader to check your work for the usual grammar, sense and spelling, but you will always be the one in control and you will have the final say regarding what is included in your book.)

"If you want to get rich from writing, write the sort of thing that's read by persons who move their lips when they're reading to themselves."

Don Marquis

EXCUSE IV:

NO – ONE'S GOING TO BUY MY BOOK!

What if I don't have a marketable idea ?

Again, the idea that you must be able to **sell** the book comes from the belief that you have to ensure that the publisher will get back their investment in you.

Let's be upfront and clear about this from the outset. The main objective of writing and publishing your authority book is not to generate income through book sales!

You **can** sell your book, but you will not become rich from the profits.

Very few authors do. In fact, a traditionally – published, commercially **successful** book will generate royalties in the region of 7% for the author.

Self – publishing actually allows you to keep more of the profits, if you do decide to offer your book for sale, but that's not the main objective, in fact it doesn't even have to be a factor.

The most important point to bear in mind is that the aim of your book is not to find buyers, but to establish you as a thought leader in your niche and showcase your services to the people you want to work with.

One of the advantages of self – publishing on the Amazon platform is that each book is printed to order – so there's no need to invest in an initial print run, or risk being stuck with a pile of unsold copies!

EXCUSE V

IT TAKES TOO LONG TO WRITE
AND PUBLISH A BOOK

If you go with a publishing house, the time from having your idea or outline accepted, to seeing your book hit the shelves is typically 18 months. Start looking for a publishing agent today, and you could be looking to print next year or the year after!

Hardly fresh content!

In addition, it's hard to get motivated and excited about a project that will only come to fruition in the long term. In fact, like most long – term projects, it is likely to take even longer as it will often be side – lined in favour of more pressing concerns.

Self – publishing allows you to get your book printed in **weeks.** Having a publication date in clear view creates motivation and momentum. Your content will be bang up – to – date and relevant, in fact your book marketing strategy can begin right at the outset!

This brings us to the key difference between traditional and self – publishing.

In traditional publishing, the publishing house directs the

book marketing. In fact, many writers, who are nervous about advertising or promoting their work, are happy to hand over the marketing strategy and planning to the publishing house. Their position is that they are quite confident of the writing process but reluctant to get involved in the marketing.

However, your objectives are likely to be the opposite when publishing your authority book. You can see how to market your book and will be reluctant to hand over control of the marketing strategy – you just need some guidance through the writing.

"What no wife of a writer can ever understand is that a writer is working when he's staring out of the window. "

Burton Rascoe

CHAPTER 4:

I DON'T KNOW WHERE TO START!

I hope by now you are beginning to realise that there really are no limitations to publishing your authority book on your terms. As you discover the incredible possibilities available to you, the opportunities to showcase your unique expertise and the services you offer, you will see the enormous potential of a published book to raise your profile, get more speaking engagements and get your work in front of your ideal clients.

You now know the advantages of self – publishing, so there are only three remaining excuses to address:

1. I've never done it before – I don't know where to start.

   I need **a proven process**.

2. I don't know who I could get to help me.

I need the **expertise** of someone who has done it before.

3. I'm too busy.

I need to get published in the **shortest time possible**.

How a Publishing Coach Can Help

I am a b2b copywriter, editor and publication coach. I have self – published my own books and guided many others through the process.

My job is not just to orchestrate the process and coach you through to publication on time, but also to guide you through the process of understanding what you want to achieve with an authority book.

It is my job to ensure that your book distills the essence of who you are and what sets you apart, and to present your unique message clearly and succinctly.

I know that there are many demands on your time and so I have optimized the publication process to allow you to get your book published in the shortest time possible with minimal interruption to your schedule.

The publishing process can take as long as you wish, but

since procrastination is perhaps the most famous and effective thief of time, my approach is to coordinate the various stages to reduce delays and to avoid self – sabotage, such as writer's block.

I work with you to keep momentum and motivation high, and to ensure that the content is fresh and relevant at the time of publication.

It is important to sustain the level of enthusiasm you generate at the time of writing, so that it will carry you through to the crucial marketing phase.

It's perfectly possible to begin marketing your book at the same time as the manuscript passes through the publication stages.

The actual process can be completed in 60 days, but your involvement in that can be pared back to a minimum. You can have as much input as you wish, or just submit the text and I will handle the rest of the project.

The hiring and coordination of an editor, proof – reader, formatter and graphic artist (for the cover) is my responsibility.

Overleaf is an example of a typical publication schedule.

Your publication schedule may be different, depending on

your specific project, but we will still aim to publish your book in 60 days or less.

DAY	YOUR INPUT	My Input
0	Coaching Session 1 (45 mins)	
1 – 7	Brainstorm ideas, gather materials. Contact the writer of the Foreword.	
8	Coaching Session 2 (45 mins)	Your Logo/Colours
9 – 18	Writing 7 – 10 days	Author Bio/Photo
19 – 23		First Edit
24 – 27	Re – write	Jacket design
28 – 31		Second Edit
31	Your sign – off	Jacket finalisation
32		My sign – off
33 – 36		Proof reading
37 – 41		Formatting + Submission to Amazon
43		Proof copies ordered
47 – 50	Final proofing	
52		Final copies ordered
56 – 60	Publication – Book in Hand	

As you can see, there is some generous time allocation to allow for any unforeseen emergencies.

In the Coaching Sessions we work together to decide on the approach and get clear on the marketing objectives of your book.

In the chapters that follow, we look at the logistics of the publication process, and at ways to get your content written quickly.

CHAPTER 5 WHY PUBLISH ON AMAZON?

COMPLETE CONTROL OVER
THE CONTENT

There are many self – publishing options available, but probably most powerful and accessible is the option offered by Amazon.

This platform allows you to upload your book content, add a cover and sell your finished book directly from the Amazon websites.

You can choose the template size, design a cover to your specifications, set the price and have Amazon assign a unique ISBN number to your finished book.

Each copy of the book is printed to order. Whenever someone buys the book online, Amazon prints a copy and the printing and postage costs are deducted from the sales price of the book.

There is no need to order an advance print run, or to estimate demand.

You piggy – back the promotional features of the world's largest book retailer to target the precise market for your book, locally or world – wide, and enjoy the convenience of their shipping and handling, distribution and returns services.

You could even distribute entirely from Amazon, without ever having to touch a physical copy of the book.

Once your book is listed on Amazon, you can display an image of the book cover and embed a link on your website, LinkedIn profile, or Facebook Fan Page, to take the reader directly to the sales page.

Amazon also lets you buy copies of the book at cost price – you just pay for the printing, postage and packaging of as many or as few copies as you like. You are not obliged to buy a set number of copies – Amazon charges the same printing price per copy whether you buy one or one thousand copies, although, obviously, shipping costs per copy will vary slightly, depending on the order size.

In the world of traditional publishing, your book will be distributed and advertised while it is selling well. As sales drop off, the publisher will stop actively distributing your book. Any unsold copies remaining will be heavily discounted and there is the very real possibility that your hard – earned efforts will go out of print and no longer be available.

In addition, any updates or corrections which appear after going to press will have to wait until the second print run or second edition of the book. If the demand for your book is not large, there is the possibility that neither of these events will actually happen. In that case, your authority book remains uncorrected, or with a corrigendum slip inserted, or becomes obsolete and irrelevant quite quickly.

Self – publishing lets you keep the content fresh and puts you in charge of the distribution.

On Amazon, you can upload corrected manuscripts or issue an updated edition at any time. Of course, it is wise to update the cover and call it a Second Edition, but that only involves re – designing the cover – not publishing a new book from scratch!

Incorporated on the Amazon websites are powerful search engine filters which allow your book to be categorized by exact niche and audience and presented to the audience you wish to target.

You choose the marketing copy – the description that

accompanies the book on the site – and you select the keywords which help your target audience to discover your title.

There is no need to order or invest in a large print run or estimate how many books will be sold. When your book appears on the Amazon site, it is available to order almost anywhere in the World. When a customer orders a book, it is printed at Amazon's printer in the United States or Europe and sent directly to the buyer. The buyer pays for the postage and packaging. The cost of printing is deducted from the sale of the book.

As the author, you also have the option to buy copies of the book at cost price – the cost of printing plus postage.

The list price of the book is decided by you, and you have the option to offer it at a discount price in promotions, if required.

Depending on the size of the book and the number of copies you order at one time, the cost of ordering copies for direct offline marketing can be optimized, to keep the price per copy affordable – often on a par with the cost of a good quality business card!

Amazon takes care of the rest – the printing, distribution, mailing prices and returns, without any input required from you.

"I love being a writer. What I can't stand is the paperwork."

Peter De Vries

CHAPTER 6 : LOGISTICS:

OPTIMIZING THE BOOK FORMAT FOR YOUR MARKETING OBJECTIVES

The Amazon publishing platform allows you to choose the format, interior and cover to suit the content and how you wish to market it.

You can choose from a range of standard template formats from 5" x 8" to 8.5" x 11".

The size of the book you decide to publish is determined by the type of content you wish to produce and how much you wish to spend per printed copy.

If your book requires detailed figures or diagrams, a larger format may be necessary to show off the detail to good effect, but for most purposes, the standard 8 x 5 and 9 x 6 formats work best.

In order to be able to print your title on the spine, it is best to aim for around 100 pages.

This book you are reading now is a standard 9" x 6" format, printed on white paper, and a glossy finish to the cover, with an interior file of approximately 100 pages.

There are options to select cream paper for the interior and a matt finish for the cover, but I think you'll agree that this option works well for business marketing purposes.

You can also opt for full colour printing in the interior file, but that will increase the printing cost per copy for the book.

With the consideration of a minimum thickness to print on the spine, 100 pages is the sweet spot to deliver maximum content for the best price.

If your book runs to fewer pages, you may not be able to display the title on the spine, but that is a minor consideration. As you go over 110 pages, you will see costs rise very slightly.

Both this format and the smaller 'pocket – sized' 8 x 5, come in at around $2.15* per copy to print. This price per copy is the same whether you order one copy or one thousand!

The cost of ordering copies to be delivered directly to you

depends on the order size.

When you order around 100 copies, as the author, that works out at around $2.60* per copy to have your order printed and delivered to your home or business address by standard mail.

You pay a bit more for a smaller order, e.g. for 25 copies, somewhere in the region of $2.75* per copy.

I think you'll agree that's an incredible price to get your best work in front of the people who matter to you!

Prices correct at the time of going to press, May 2017

Note: The larger 8.5 x 11 format works well as a sales brochure and is an effective marketing tool, as a pamphlet format, without the need to print the title on the spine.

EDITING, PROOF – READING, FORMATTING

Whether you are an experienced writer or an absolute novice, it is imperative that you get a second pair of eyes to review your writing before publication.

This is your authority statement and any typing errors or glaring spelling mistakes will reflect badly on your work.

While it is virtually impossible to guarantee that no mistakes will enter the copy, it is important to implement a strategy that ensures they are eliminated as far as possible. When you are writing, you become closely entangled with your subject and you know your work so well that it becomes difficult to scrutinize the content impartially to detect errors in grammar, spelling, typing or formatting.

I act as that second pair of eyes on the look out for any mistakes that can creep into the copy. I have many years of experience in editing and proof – reading professionally, but, even so, I employ a proof – reader to give you the assurance that all care has been taken to present your content as professionally as possible.

You will have an opportunity to review the text again before formatting and publication, but, if you don't have the time or wish to trust in the publishing process, you can skip that formality knowing that the greatest care has been taken to polish the copy.

After the copy has passed these stages, it is passed to a professional formatter, who ensures that fonts and settings are consistent throughout the body of the text and that the format meets Amazon's standards for publication. This is a wise investment, to ensure that no section of the book looks out of place or sloppy and to minimise the time required to have the final proof copy approved for publication.

Once approved, the interior print file is loaded together with the cover design and submitted to Amazon to print a proof copy.

A copy will be shipped directly to your home or business address, to allow you to check everything is in order prior to publication on the Amazon website.

BOOK JACKET DESIGN

Crucial to your marketing is an attractive, professionally – designed book cover.

This can be done quite quickly and at the same time as your book content, especially if you already have the key ingredients for the layout:

1. A high – resolution profile picture, preferably taken by a professional photographer.

2. Your signature colour scheme or preferred cover colour.

3. Your unique eye – catching logo

4. An idea for a high – resolution image

5. A great title

6. An explanatory subtitle

Amazon offers a range of free book jacket templates which can be customized to a certain degree.

We can work on the cover before the book text is finalized, in order to optimize the process.

Don't worry if you don't have a logo yet; we can get that

done, too!

It is also possible to have a completely custom – designed book jacket created by a professional graphic artist. This service costs extra, depending on how much work you require, but can usually be achieved for around $200 – $300.

Fill your paper with the breathings of your heart."

William Wordsworth

CHAPTER 7 : CREATING THE CONTENT I

If you already have the outline for a book and are motivated by the possibilities and potential of self – publishing, it's only a matter of fleshing out the bones to create sufficient content for your authority book.

Logistics.

For a book of this size (6" x 9"), it requires approximately 10,000 to 12,000 words, depending on font size and layout.

This book contains approximately 10,000 words, from Foreword to 'About the Author'.

You can, of course add more content by using a smaller font, running to more pages or moving to a larger book format.

Too much Content

Personally, I don't recommend going much beyond 10,000 words for your first authority book. At this size, it's possible to read completely in a couple of hours, or skim through in less than 30 minutes – perfect to read on the plane or at a queue at the airport. At that length, there's a good chance of getting your main points read.

If you have more to say, why not keep it for your next title? Once you have published one book and become familiar with the process, it's much easier to do it again. When you see the power of marketing your book on Amazon, you will be keen to duplicate that success, and a second book gives you the opportunity to connect again with your audience, go into more detail – and, of course add testimonials from your readers to the book cover!

From a practical point of view, a larger book is harder to carry round with you and less convenient to post.

Not Enough Content

For many first time authors, the opposite problem is the case. They may have the idea or the general outline for a book, but are wondering how long it will take to compile 10,000 words.

That's not as much as it sounds. Let's break that content down into its component parts.

Let's assume you decide to go along with this format and publish 100 pages. How much content to you need to generate?

Using this model, your introductory pages (including a Foreword written by someone else!), appendices (references, index, etc.), and About the Author page will account for about 2, 500 words.

That leaves about 7,500 words to fill around 8 to 10 chapters.

So let's say 10 chapters at 750 words.

To put that in context, the recommended word count for a blogpost or post on LinkedIn comes in at around 600 words.

That's a chapter on one side of A4 paper.

Viewed like that, the challenge doesn't seem so great!

So let's look at how to get that content done as painlessly as possible.

"Everywhere I go I'm asked if I think the university stifles writers. My opinion is that they don't stifle enough of them. There's many a best — seller that could have been prevented by a good teacher."

Flannery O'Connor

CHAPTER 8: CREATING THE CONTENT II

RE – PURPOSE YOUR WHITE PAPER AND MARKETING COPY

If you already have a good quality white paper, why not put it to work for you and turn the content into a publication for a wider audience.

You already own the content and a white paper is usually quite tightly – packed with formal, factual information.

In fact the White Paper format, although the essential backbone of your B2B marketing, has several limitations when it comes to establishing your business profile in your niche.

The industry standard for a white paper expects the presentation of the **general case** for the service or product you deliver. The unspoken rule is that it does not overtly advertise you or your company as the only provider of that service – although you can, of course, add your personal logo, contact details and links to your website on the cover page, header, footer, conclusion etc.

This means that a buyer or potential client often views a batch of white papers from similar providers and makes a decision to work with you or someone else based on other marketing channels.

The White Paper is not a forum to showcase what makes you unique and the particular aspects of your service that you wish to highlight.

If you wish to establish yourself as a leading player in developing, implementing or delivering the service, your white paper is simply the factual evidence for the service provided by you or your business.

A typical white paper is in the region of 2, 500 to 4,000 words. If you adapt this factual information to form the framework of your book, you could probably find you have around 5,000 to 6,000 words when the tight copy is expanded into a less formal, more accessible style for a general audience.

If this is then supplemented by other marketing materials you already have, you can see how quickly you can assemble 7,000 words to form the main body of your book.

Examples of existing marketing content could be sales

brochures, a case study which details how you delivered your service successfully to a satisfied customer*, or outlines of how you offered a range of services to different customers.

You have space to expand on your particular experience or know – how and to explain precisely why your solution is particularly powerful or effective.

Unlike the white paper format, you can stamp your personality on your work and show what sets you apart or what is different about how you deliver your solution.

People work with people they like – people who are like them. The more you describe who you are, the more likely you are to resonate with your ideal clients – the clients you would love to work with!

*The case study and testimonials will require permission from the clients. However, this will be easier to obtain if you can show them how inclusion in your book can result in more publicity for them or their company. Offer to include a link to their website – and, of course, promise them a free copy of the published book!

CHAPTER 9: CREATING THE CONTENT III: EXISTING POSTS FROM YOUR WEBSITE OR SOCIAL MEDIA PAGES

Any content you have already published online can be effectively re – purposed to showcase your work and your services. Just remember the power of Google to pick up on duplicate content, so be careful not to repeat content *verbatim* when you come to marketing the book online.

Other than that, the thought of publishing 10 blog posts seems much less daunting than sitting down to write a book!

Begin with 10 compelling chapter titles, then summarise the points you want to make under each. That way you can easily organize what you want to say into a logical order.

The chapters can either be used to unfold the argument in a logical sequence, or they can be stand – alone units.

Either way, you should list the chapter titles at the front of the book and, if necessary, add an index at the back of the book.

Any references you make to previously published work can be included as a Appendix.

CHAPTER 10
WRITING OPTIONS

If you are passionate about your message and the service you deliver, your head is probably buzzing with all the thoughts and ideas you would like to present in the book.

However, knowing where to start and actually sitting down to get those thoughts on paper can be overwhelming.

If the fear of the blank page is stopping you getting your message in print, there are some simple hacks to get over the hurdles to get it done.

"Perfectionism is the Mother of Procrastination."

1. Get over the perfectionism. Yes, this book reflects you, and so you want to present your best work to the World.

    However, you don't need to capture the complexity of you in one volume! If you feel compelled to include everything and are frightened of missing something, you will severely limit your ability to get published quickly. Beware of those subtle tricks of the subconscious mind to present you with excuses for delaying publication and avoiding change!

Two of the great features of self – publishing on Amazon, which help you to avoid the trap of perfectionism, are :

(i)   You can always edit or update drafts of the book on the Amazon platform, so you can correct any errors that creep in. Also, if you need to add an amendment or adjust, delete, expand on any area, you can simply launch a second edition. This is especially useful if you are in a field which is changing quickly. Unlike a traditional book, where publishers don't update until the first print run is sold, you have the opportunity to keep your content fresh and up – to – date. For a second edition, you design a new cover and have another opportunity to present your work to your audience.

(ii)   Once you have published a book and overcome the 'newness' of the experience, it becomes much easier to write a second and a third. As you think about getting your first book written, you can see where some subjects might work well as a stand – alone book – and the pressure is off to cram everything into one volume.

2. Don't try to write it as a continuous text. Chunk it up into bite sized pieces. Start with the chapter headings. What subjects do you want to talk about?

3. When you know which 8 to 10 subjects you intend to address, a useful tip is to take a sheet of A4 paper for each title. You can use 10 files on your computer, but the paper route is much more visual, enabling you to see the overall picture.

   Spread the sheets out on a table in front of you.

4. Write a chapter number and title on each sheet. Then just brainstorm subjects you want to talk about and assign each subject to the appropriate chapter.

HATE WRITING OR DON'T HAVE TIME

Dictate the content for each chapter on your smart phone, tablet or any recording device.

Sometimes it is easier to talk about what you do – and it should be easy to talk about your specialist subject – you and your unique service.

Don't attempt to dictate huge speeches at once.

Bear in mind that a typical chapter will contain between 750 and one thousand words.

Depending on how fast you speak and the number of pauses or repetitions you include, typical dictation speed is around 120 words a minute.

Write down your chapter headings, break each chapter into 2 or 3 sections. Then dictate short, 2 to 3 minute, recordings on each subject.

To transcribe your mp3 files into printed form, you can use a service like www.transcribeme.com. They charge around $0.79 per minute for 90 – 95% accuracy – recommended if you intend to edit the printed form yourself and $2.00 per minute for greater than 99% accuracy.

This way you could dictate and print an entire book,

without having to do any writing at all, and requiring as little as 3 hours of your time!

At that stage simply send me the typed script and the recording files, and let me take care of the rest.

THE NEXT STEP: GETTING STARTED

When you are ready to take the next step, simply contact me here:

Ruth@ruthesullivan.com

My initial consultation is free, and can be scheduled from my website. You can opt for a telephone conversation or Skype call.

I look forward to hearing from you!

ABOUT THE AUTHOR

Ruth Sullivan has been writing, editing publishing and consulting for over 30 years. A graduate of the University of St Andrews, in the United Kingdom, she has extensive experience in UK industry and International Organisations.

Her knowledge of b2b copywriting, marketing, coaching and consulting is invaluable in publishing books for the purpose of establishing author authority.

She divides her time between Italy, France and Great Britain.

For further information or to schedule a strategy session, please go to www.ruthesullivan.com

www.ingramcontent.com/pod-product-compliance
Lightning Source LLC
Chambersburg PA
CBHW051733170526
45167CB00002B/920